P's & Q's
FOR PROFIT

Lewena Bayer and Karen Mallett

GREAT PLAINS
PUBLICATIONS

Great Plains Publications
3–161 Stafford Street
Winnipeg, MB R3M 2W9
www.greatplains.mb.ca

Great Plains Publications gratefully acknowledges the financial support
provided for its publishing program by the Government of Canada
through the Book Publishing Industry Development Program (BPIDP).

Design & Typography by Gallant Design Ltd.
Printed in Canada by Kromar Printing Ltd.

CANADIAN CATALOGUING IN PUBLICATION DATA

Bayer, Lewena

P's & Q's for profit

       (In good company ; 2)

       ISBN 1-894283-21-X

I.   Business etiquette.   I. Mallett, Karen.

II. Title.   III. Series: Bayer, Lewena. In good company ; 2

HF5389.B38 2001   395.5'2   C2001-910162-7

To Anne and Bruce Knicley who as parents gave me their encouragement and strength to find my way to being myself.

Karen

To my parents, Ted and Linda Sheard, who taught me long ago that "grace" was more than prayer at dinnertime.

Lewena

Table of Contents

INTRODUCTION

Effective communications are the bedrock of modern business. With new technologies constantly being developed, we now have many ways to communicate, from telephones to pagers to emails to voicemails to faxes to video conferencing to plain old face-to-face meetings. And we use most of them every day. But even though the modes, quantity, and reliability of our communication have advanced at a rapid pace, the quality of our communication has deteriorated. Most of us just aren't sure what the modern etiquette guidelines are. As a result, we resort to sloppy, slang-filled speech about mundane and inappropriate topics, we send emails with no return address and expect people to know who they're from, we spell-check our correspondence but forget to proofread it, we confuse social and business interactions and find ourselves the laughing stock of the office Christmas party even as we're crying our way out the door. Careless communication has a price. Whether you're writing a cover letter for that dream job, doing a presentation for a key client, or meeting your future boss for lunch, you'll want to present yourself positively and politely. Communication is key.

Ironically, it's good old-fashioned etiquette that is the key to success in an ultra-modern business environment. Once perceived as "soft skills," how you communicate with others through your attire, attitude, demeanor and conduct has become increasingly more important. From creating a successful and confident physical presence to writing clearly and concisely, courteous behaviors are often the prerequisites for the skills that get us a job, a promotion, a client base, and determine success in modern business. P's & Q's are not just for the profit of an individual seeking a job or promotion, but also for the profit of the company itself.

Whether you're looking for a job, looking to move up the corporate ladder, or looking to improve your rapport with clients, how you present yourself, how you speak, and how you conduct yourself are as important as your knowledge and education. Mannerful behaviors are invaluable in first acquiring, and then keeping your dream job, getting past the "gatekeeper" or selling to that key client. *P's and Q's for Profit* validates the old adage of "mind your business" and aptly equates it to "mind your manners." The book presents guidelines for modern business behavior in verbal communications, interviews both for and on the job, written correspondence, meetings, and mixed social and business functions. These guidelines will help you present a confident, competent image in any business situation. But it's not enough to understand "the rules," you have to practise them. And, with every action, make a sincere effort to respect yourself. In doing so, you'll show respect for others. The rewards will follow, and yes, you'll see how P's and Q's can positively affect the bottom line.

Chapter One

IN THE BEGINNING WAS THE WORD:
Verbal and non-verbal communications

alk, talk, talk. Ever wondered how many words you say in a day? Wouldn't it be interesting to know what ratio of "talk" is in-person versus how much is over the phone or via the computer? There's no doubt that the quantity of "talking" we're doing in print has increased substantially, but a phone call is still better than an email, and an in-person meeting is better yet. Whether it's on the phone or face-to-face, our speech, tone and body language communicate a first impression that tells potential employers, clients, and higher-ups that we are professional, prepared, and profitable business people.

How are your verbal and non-verbal skills? Take the self-assessment on the following page and find out.

I really feel like we're communicating here.

Quiz: Self-assessment

	True or False
1. You have 5 minutes to make a first impression.	
2. Studies show that up to 50 per cent of the message received by someone when you're speaking is non-verbal.	
3. People are more likely to trust you when they first meet you if they can see both your hands.	
4. When you shake someone's hand it's appropriate to move your body in close proximity to theirs and it's okay to pat them or put your other hand on their elbow or shoulder.	
5. When someone says, "Don't get up!", they really mean it and it's not necessary to get up.	
6. If you're meeting two or more co-workers at the same time, you should always introduce yourself and shake hands with the women first.	
7. When public speaking, it's not really important to look anyone in particular in the eye. Just glancing up from your notes occasionally will suffice.	
8. It's very important to modify your speech style and the type of language you use when meeting different people.	
9. The objective of first impressions is to determine whether you trust someone enough to continue a relationship with them.	
10. People appreciate a clean and neat appearance, however, they will notice your attitude and demeanor more than they'll notice your clothes.	

(See answers at the end of this chapter.)

A. Know what you want: Preparing for business interactions

How can you be sure you are communicating a positive impression of yourself to others? Well, for starters, it's probably a good idea to know for certain what you want to say. For example, if you want to portray competence, your attitude, gestures, overt behavior, and the words that come out of your mouth should all portray competence. The slightest discrepancy in any area will be noticed and judged distrustful by others. Communicating with care requires preparation and attention to detail.

Let's say that "success" is epitomized by the following traits:

- competence
- authority
- credibility
- self-confidence
- responsibility
- trustworthiness

How does one communicate these characteristics to others? Certainly, how we look, dress and move sends an overt message. But how do we purposefully communicate these traits intelligibly through our every interaction? Think about this. Visualize what "competence" looks like, speaks like, and walks like.

B. I said it through the grapevine: Speaking clearly

When we are speaking to others, content is important, but so is clarity. Speaking too quickly, being too quiet or too loud, using words others don't understand, and many other obstacles prevent us from getting our message across and can turn the best content into mumbo jumbo. When you speak, remember to keep it slow and simple, say all of your words, take pauses, keep your tone and volume consistent, and most importantly, pay attention to see that others are listening.

Here are some common misconceptions about speaking:

- If you cannot be understood, speak louder.
- If you want to communicate a lot of information in a short period of time, speak faster.
- If you continually tell stories about your fascinating life, you will be the hit of every work function.
- You should memorize really big words and use them whenever possible so your associates will think you're smart.
- When others do not agree with you, debate with them until they see your point of view, and never give up.
- If someone is speaking slowly or pauses a lot, help them out by finishing their sentences for them.
- As long as you nod your head or say the occasional "mm hmm," no one will know that you're not really listening.
- Using in-house acronyms or business lingo will impress people from other companies.
- If you ask questions that stump your peer group or, even better, your superiors, everyone will be impressed with you.

Remember, the point of speaking is to communicate content, not to impress, confuse, or irritate others!

C. Trust me: Matching your words to your body language

The first seconds of every interaction are vital. When we meet someone new, or initially hear a voice on the phone, we make judgments about others and they make judgments about us. In business, these judgments determine whether we trust a person enough to do business with them. Mistrust occurs when communication signals don't match. For example, your words are friendly but your tone is not. Your presentation materials are professional but your attire is sloppy and your body language says nervousness. What you say may seem true enough, but your failure to make eye contact communicates insincerity.

Practise matching your words, deportment, speech style, and non-verbal cues to ensure you are sending clear and concise messages. Following these simple steps will help ensure that your gestures and non-verbal behaviors match what's coming out or your mouth:

- Practise your posture. Stand with your feet slightly apart, shoulders back and chin forward. When you're engaged in a conversation, stand still. Don't fidget, and keep your hands by your side.

- Maintain eye contact. Don't let your eyes wander as your head typically follows. If you're uncomfortable looking directly at the person you're talking to, look at their eyebrows.

- Try to focus on the communication at hand. Think about something positive. If you're in a bad mood, at least your smile will be sincere.

- If you cannot be genuine in your interaction, let the person know it's not a good time to talk, or ask them to come back later. The last thing you want to do is give a bad impression to an important client.

Certainly we can all describe examples of people we know who do not send a message of success. May we introduce:

SLOPPY JOE: It's pretty darned obvious that Sloppy Joe either just got out of bed and didn't have time to change, or he didn't go home at all. You'd think a guy would be on time for his own meeting. Who would feel comfortable paying this guy to make presentations on behalf of their company? Sloppy clothes, sloppy attitude, sloppy language… Thank goodness it wasn't a lunch meeting, one can only imagine how he eats!

THE NAMEDROPPER: Someone should tell the name-dropper that sitting in the same restaurant as a local celebrity is hardly the same as actually meeting them. Why would anyone care if Dr. Zhivago's daughter lives next door to him at the lake? Why would anyone want to know that his cousin is dating the lawyer that represents Burton Cummings?

THE SPINDOCTOR: The last time you talked to the spin doctor, she said she knew your boss really well. Funny, Mr. Boss has never heard of her. Strange too, she insinuated she'd been at the company for ten years, but it's only been ten months. Whatever you do, divide everything she says by three and then consider believing half of it.

Oh yes, we've worked together forever...

D. Talking headiquette: How to get people involved in conversation

Have you ever been engaged in conversation with someone who continuously nods their head while looking at you with eyebrows raised and an occasional half-smile? Head bobbing typically means one of three things: you've failed to engage them in what you are saying, they don't know what you're talking about but are too embarrassed to ask, or you're talking so much that you've become a blurred, mumbling head.

Polite conversation is a two-way street. Someone talks briefly, while someone else listens intently. At some point, the speaker usually signals that it's the listener's turn to talk by asking them a question. Speaker and listener switch roles and the process is repeated resulting in a conversation. Seems simple enough, but there's a little more to the art of conversation. Here are some tips on how to get the most out of business conversation:

- **Don't let your mouth do the thinking:** How often has something just run out of your mouth before you even realized you were thinking it, never mind saying it out loud? We suggest you say it in your head first. If it makes sense and seems appropriate, only then can you say it out loud. The resulting pauses can give the impression that intelligent commentary will follow, and this encourages others to pay attention.

- **Listen:** You can learn a great deal by listening and, if you actually pay attention to what is being said, you may actually benefit from the conversation. Ask questions that show interest in the speaker and their topic. Remember, the best conversationalist is a good listener.

- **Don't interrupt:** Interruptions are always seen as disrespectful and can also be seen as "one-upmanship." If you have an idea that you are enthusiastic about communicating, wait for a pause from the speaker, or better yet, ask if you can speak.

- **Tell the truth:** Stick to the real story. Remember that if you're not being completely honest, your gestures, tone of voice, and speech style are not going to match the words coming out of your mouth. Avoid topics that make you feel less than confident, and don't pretend to know something you don't.

- **Be consistent:** Consistency is an aspect of professionalism, so show it in your everyday speech. Don't change the way you talk depending on where you are or with whom you're speaking. People respect consistency in business.

- **Keep it simple:** Use words that others understand and that help to improve the direction and tone of the conversation. This does not mean you have to use simple words during all discussions, but making up words or using them out of context will only make you look silly.

- **Respect other's opinions:** Keep all of the people in your group involved with the conversation by asking for their opinion. Always remember that an opinion is merely an opinion, and being right is not always part of the equation.

■ **Be positive:** Compliment others on their ideas and keep the conversation as positive as possible.

When we are more concerned with talking than listening, any conversation can become a communication catastrophe. As soon as we start to pay attention to what others say and show consideration by giving them our full attention, it is amazing what can be accomplished.

E. Mind your business: Avoiding overly familiar speech

In a business environment, professionalism is the key to gaining respect and trust from co-workers and clients. Familiarity can, indeed, breed contempt. Worse, being overly familiar with co-workers can cause lazy habits that spill over into your meetings with clients, bosses, and others who do not know you as well as your co-workers do. The best insurance against becoming overly casual is maintaining professional standards at all times. Here are some important rules for dealing with business associates:

■ **Avoid the "chicken run" of foul language:** How often have you been caught off guard by foul language that just slips out? Sometimes people will use four-letter words for impact or to get someone's full attention. Using foul language amongst your peer group at work insinuates that there is a certain level of comfort and bonding happening. However, complaints about swearing often go unspoken and the opposite of bonding is actually happening. If a message is appropriately and completely prepared, foul language will not be required in any business situation. And the less often you use foul language, darn it, the less likely it will be to slip out when you're not expecting it!

- **Err on the formal side:** In most business situations, reversion to easy, common language is interpreted as lazy and unprofessional. Avoid dropping consonants, slurring the ends of sentences, mumbling, or reverting to slang. Always try to speak slowly and clearly while maintaining an even pitch. Practise speaking into a tape recorder. Try to avoid saying "um," and make a point of saying every syllable in every word. Do not use vulgar language, euphemisms and jargon. Always be direct and use real words.

- **No need to entertain:** Becoming too comfortable in initial business settings can result in others not taking you seriously. Be careful with humor, don't force laughter and don't take on the responsibility of entertainer.

- **Don't gossip:** Be careful not to give too much unnecessary information, and choose appropriate topics. If someone you've known for all of fifteen minutes already knows that you have psoriasis, that your cat's name is Mousy, that you can't stand the smell of broccoli cooking, and that there's a girl in your office named Joanne who is unmarried and pregnant, you are talking too much and very unprofessionally.

F. Chapter summary

First impressions are vital to any initial business communication. Speaking clearly, developing good listening skills, making sure your speech, tone and body language match, and maintaining professionalism are the keys to presenting yourself positively.

Remember that manners are about making others comfortable in your company. A firm handshake, a smile and maintaining eye contact are a great start for an initial meeting. Be prepared with various topics that are industry-related or focus on others by asking questions about the organizations or people in the room. There is no need to be overly familiar, but you can still be yourself. Sincerity will keep you relaxed yet confident.

Answers to self-assessment quiz

1. **False.** 15-60 seconds only. Make them count!

2. **True.** Some studies show that up to 55 per cent is non-verbal message, only 7 per cent is the actually words spoken and the remaining 38 per cent is actually messages interpreted through tone of voice.

3. **True.** For whatever reason, people like to see your hands.

4. **False.** Yes, it's correct that you should move your body towards them, but don't get too close and try to resist putting your hands on them.

5. **False.** Regardless of the circumstances, it shows respect to stand when you meet someone. If a desk or something is between you, come out from behind it.

6. **False.** In business, rank determines everything, gender does not play a role. You would introduce everyone by saying the highest ranking individual's name first and you would shake hands with everyone in the order that they are introduced to you. If it is unclear who is high rank, simply smile, introduce yourself, offer your hand and typically the highest in rank will take over.

7. **False.** At some point you should make eye contact with the audience. Smile at someone at least. If lighting and spacing prohibit direct eye contact, you should "skim" the room with your eyes as often as possible.

8. **True.** If you are speaking to someone outside your industry, you need to leave out jargon and "work speak" that they don't understand. Also, you often have to adjust your rate of speech to the listener's rate of listening.

9. **True.** Most often if we get a bad first impression we can hear ourselves say, "I don't know why but something about them just bothers me." First impressions are about making verbal cues match non-verbal cues which leads to a trustworthy first impression.

10. **True.** People may decide whether they initially approach you at all based on your outward appearance, however, once contact is made, your attitude and demeanor will determine whether they continue to speak with you or not.

Chapter Two

HI, HO, HI, HO, IT'S OFF TO WORK WE GO:
Interview etiquette

Nowhere is it more important to prepare and practise presenting the precise message you wish to communicate than in a formal interview setting. But one thing most people forget is that even when you've got the job, the interview isn't over! Most businesspeople are surprised to make the realization that they are actually being interviewed or interviewing continuously, even when they are not aware of it. In the business world others are always judging us. Our daily routines and interactions are often monitored and, although a formal interview has not taken place, decisions are being made during that informal exchange or observation. The clients that we may have already attained are most likely being approached by our competition. So keeping those key clients can be as labor-intensive as being successfully interviewed by new, potential clients.

So, if you could be a tree, what kind of tree would you be...

How are you in an interview? Take the quiz and find out. During this assessment, try to keep in mind that the interview may not always be for a job.

Quiz: Self-assessment

		True or False
1.	Regardless of the type of job you're applying for, you should always wear a conservative navy suit.	
2.	It is appropriate to telephone the interviewer after an interview:	
	a) immediately when you get home.	
	b) the next day if the interviewer indicated it was okay to do so.	
	c) in two weeks; you don't want to appear too anxious.	
	d) every couple of hours and leave a voicemail.	
3.	If a potential employer calls you at home, they don't expect you to act professionally on the phone because it's an informal situation.	
4.	It's better to white out an old address and get your resumé in before the deadline than to take the time to update it and have it arrive late.	
5.	If you're expecting an important call, it's okay to take your cell phone into an interview.	
6.	If you are difficult to reach, you should give the interviewer several numbers so they can try to track you down.	
7.	Even if your current employer is unaware that you are seeking new opportunities, it is okay for new employers to contact you during work hours at the company number.	

	True or False
8. You should always make a point of mentioning that one of your parents is a big corporate client of a potential employer.	
9. It is very important that you are comfortable in an interview so you should wear whatever makes you feel most confident even if it is "business casual."	
10. You should always make sure to have fresh breath in an interview, even if you have to chew gum.	

(See answers at the end of this chapter.)

A. Please sir, I want the job: Tips for making a good first impression

Don't you just dread interviews, the worrying, guessing, fidgeting and sweaty palms? Whether you've just spent $40,000 on an education and are interviewing for your dream job or you spent your last $200 on a new suit jacket, the money's wasted if you don't get the job. To leave an interview with that gut-wrenching pit in your stomach, the ache in your brain that says, I blew it: we have all been there. Here are a couple of our old friends who are consistently there and never seem to learn.

> **MONTE HALL:** Let's make a deal. "If you can show me three weeks holidays, full medical, no evening or weekend work and a corner suite with windows before I leave this interview, I will take the job." This wheeler dealer usually has the least amount of skills and experience, feels the world owes him, and although he has never held down a job, he loves to negotiate. Has no one ever taught him the difference between confidence and cockiness?

Hee, um, oh um, no-o-o-o, um, well...

NERVOUS NELLIE: The interviewee rushes into the room with a pool of sweat that has the mop-up committee working overtime. Giggles monopolize the conversation and, no matter what comments are made by the person across the table, Nervous Nellie can barely lift her head, never mind make eye contact. When the short interview ends she trips on the table leg and rushes from the room wringing her hands.

What's the secret to handling yourself properly in an interview? Remember that etiquette is about showing care and consideration for others. In an interview, that means simply taking your cues from the interviewer. If you and the interviewer share a personal acquaintance, don't bring it up unless they do. Don't ask about money or how long the interview will last unless they bring up the subject. Do follow directions. Take a chair if offered, laugh along with a joke—but no knee-slapping. Leave politics, religion, your last hot date or your grandmother's health out of the conversation. Should you take that cup of coffee? Not if you're nervous and think you might spill, and certainly not if you're going to need a half-caf, low-fat soya with no foam but extra vanilla and raw sugar. You can politely refuse. Generally, if you follow your interviewer's lead, a lot of awkward interview moments can be avoided.

Here are the top ten things to remember if you want to make a great first impression at your next interview:

1. **Be on time:** "Better late then never" does not apply during an interview. Arrive about ten minutes early so you have time to compose yourself and check your appearance. Make sure you know with whom you'll be meeting and that you've given yourself plenty of time. Introduce yourself to the receptionist or administrative person, and they will hopefully announce your arrival.

2. **Dress appropriately:** Make sure you look the part for which you are applying. Inappropriate attire will take the interviewer by surprise and can be quite distracting. The "hot date" outfit should be left for another time. A classic suit in a neutral color is always a safe bet. In preparation for the interview, you should certainly research the company and the position and dress accordingly.

3. **Greet with confidence:** Stand up straight and smile when you first meet the interviewer. Make eye contact and extend your hand. A proper handshake is three pumps from the elbow, firm, but not bone-crushing. In modern business arenas, a handshake is the only acceptable greeting and a proper handshake exhibits confidence and respect for others.

4. **Be prepared:** Eat something before you go so that a rumbling stomach does not interrupt you. Make sure you have a pen, an extra copy of your resumé and quick access to updated reference information. Remember to plug the parking meter; an interruption during this meeting could be fatal. And make sure you've prepared a mental list of your expectations, relevant accomplishments and some pertinent questions about the position or the company. This shows you've done your research.

5. **Be professional:** Do not be overly personal with the interviewer and do not discuss issues unrelated to the job at hand. It is not necessary to compliment the interviewer's appearance, name drop, or ask them personal questions. Answer questions that are asked of you in a brief but concise manner and do not give unnecessary information.

6. **Pay attention:** Turn off your cell phone or pager. Focus, do not yawn, fidget or act like you have to be somewhere else. Give the interviewer your undivided attention. Body language and non-verbal communication speak volumes.

7. **Don't panic:** A well thought-out answer is more impressive than an entertaining but irrelevant anecdote. Before you answer a tough question, take a deep breath, organize your thoughts and if necessary, ask to come back to the question later. (Hopefully they'll forget!) Don't pretend to know something you don't.

8. **Don't embellish:** It can be tempting to overstate the truth when you're trying to make yourself look good, but resist! Someone always knows someone from somewhere who can or cannot verify your story. You don't want to get caught in a lie.

9. **Be positive:** Don't badmouth current or past employers. There is always something positive you can say and employers will be impressed by your good manners and discretion.

10. **Don't be demanding:** Unless you're a very lucky person who was specially called upon by the company to work for them, remember you're asking THEM for a job. So don't express your "terms" in a first interview, that is, tell an interviewer you will not work after 5:00pm, ever, or that you are allergic to polyester uniforms and you have to eat at 12:00 sharp to keep your biorhythms in line. They're not here to meet your demands.

B. Prepare yourself: Etiquette for different types of interviews

Modern business puts people in all kinds of unique scenarios, from new technology to social/business situations, that require good old-fashioned etiquette to see you through. Nowhere is this more evident than in the multitude of different interview settings in which you might find yourself. Good etiquette can carry you through any type of interview. Here are a some tips for a multitude of interview scenarios:

- **Panel:** A group of people sitting across a table from you asking you alternate questions, what could be scarier? If you greet each one, make eye contact and smile at all throughout the interview, you'll find yourself facing several individuals, not a group, and you won't be so overwhelmed. Don't forget to shake hands with each when you leave.

- **Telephone:** Sometimes they'll purposely call when you least expect it to see how you handle yourself. If you always use good telephone etiquette, you'll never be caught off guard. Keep your resumé by the phone, let housemates know you may be getting a call, and ask the caller to "hold for one minute" while you change to a private phone and get yourself prepared.

- **Chain:** Getting called back for several interviews is a sign you're a likely candidate for the job. Here's where listening pays off. If you pay close attention to each successive interviewer, you'll be able determine what they want. Also, practise summarizing your employment history and goals in a few sentences to reiterate to each new person you meet.

- **Presentation:** If you are asked to prepare a short presentation for the interview, keep it short! If you try to be concise in all your business communications, this will come easily for you. Say what you mean and mean what you say. And, most importantly, practise, practise, practise!

- **Video:** Sometimes you may be asked to send a tape of yourself to an interviewer in another city. Treat this interview as though you were face-to-face with the interviewer in a formal office setting. Dress appropriately and make sure your leftover dishes and ZZ Top poster are not in view of the camera. Watch your tone of voice and your body language. Remember, you're sending a first impression.

- **Email:** This is becoming a common method of interviewing. Here are three basic etiquette guidelines for email interviews:

  1. Follow directions. Send your resumé in the format requested and fill in all the blanks. Just as you would not put a line through an application and write "see resumé" on top, you should never skip the fill in portions of an online application. It's no different than answering questions in an in-person interview; you wouldn't skip a question and ask the interviewer to go on, and you wouldn't say "it's in my resumé" when they asked you a question.

  2. Check your return address. Can you imagine the human resources person at a major bank seriously considering your application if your email address is baby@bootieforhire.com? Just as you wouldn't walk into an interview in a baby-doll t-shirt, don't present your written-self as anything less than confident and serious about your work.

  3. Proofread! Spelling and grammar do matter. Make sure your address and telephone number are accurate. Good etiquette requires the same clarity and consideration when we write as when we speak.

- **Personality Test/Aptitude:** If you are required to take assessment tests, be a good sport and take them, even if you think they're stupid. And don't cheat; you're probably being monitored!

- **On the job:** If you've acquired good etiquette skills that you practise all the time, this type of interview should be a breeze.

- **Luncheon:** Brush up on your table manners! That way you'll be able to focus on the interview aspect of the lunch without worrying about spilling on yourself or using the wrong fork. Other than food being involved, this is a formal interview. Don't let the casual surroundings fool you.

- **Reception:** Just like a luncheon, this interview format is really a social skills test. The interviewer is looking for professionalism and comfort in social/business situations. They want to feel comfortable having you interact with their clients. Practise your handshake and mingle! Whatever you do, don't hang out by the shrimp tree and maybe avoid that second drink, especially if you're nervous. Above all, think before you speak. That man you told the dirty joke to in the elevator on the way up could be the CEO you haven't met yet.

So...this nun went into a bar...

C. Ask me anything: Using etiquette to get through tough questions

Etiquette is useful in tricky interview situations where questions are vague and not job specific. In giving answers, use the basics of good communication you learned in Chapter One. Your interviewer is looking for these traits in you:

- competence
- authority
- credibility
- self-confidence
- responsibility
- trustworthiness

Here are some of the most commonly asked questions and what the interviewer is looking for:

Q: **Why are you the best candidate for the job?**

A: **Competence:** Your answer should reflect your ability to understand the job you are applying for. Cite examples that relate to the position you want. Telling them you are great and love people is not going to help them determine your competence.

Q: **Tell me about a difficult situation you've encountered with a client in your previous job and how you handled it.**

A: **Authority:** Keep answers positive and have the ending work out favorably. Showing that you can handle criticism, initiate results rather than waiting for others to do so, or simply showing that you can turn around a difficult situation will give you a mature and confident air.

Q: **What are your weaknesses?**

A: **Self-confidence:** This commonly asked question can make all of us dig deep in that pile of negative thoughts and make us pull out answers that can have an interviewer saying, "Don't let the door hit you on the way out." Citing a weakness that you have overcome, is a way of showing confidence; after all, only a brave person can admit when they are weak. For example, if you are not a great delegator, try saying something like this: "I used to find myself working overtime to get assignments done rather than trusting others to do the work so I took a course on time management and responsible delegation which has helped me tremendously." You get the picture, be human and then be super human.

Q: **What is your greatest accomplishment?**

A: **Credibility:** There's a great temptation to embellish here, but simplicity is always best. Remember to be professional, concise, and to say what you mean. And most importantly, tell the truth. You don't want to get caught out in a lie!

Q: What would your closest friends tell me about you?

A: **Trustworthiness:** The interviewer is asking for one word attributes that reflect trustworthiness. Try loyal, honest, determined, positive, reliable and confident.

Q: Tell me what you liked and disliked about your last job?

A: **Responsibility:** Good etiquette requires never talking about people behind their back so, first and foremost, never openly criticize a client, boss or co-worker. When discussing dislikes, use answers that relate to your own goals, such as "I wanted to move into a certain area and the job required me to move in a different direction."

Q: If you could be a piece of fruit what would you be?

A: **Lunacy:** OK that might be a bit dramatic but do you really want to work for someone who is picturing you as a ripe peach or a firm banana?

D. In reference to what? Protocol for using references

If you keep good manners in mind, you'll never go wrong with references. That's because you'll remember that your references deserve to be shown consideration. That means you phone them in advance to check that it is okay to use them, to let them know someone might be calling, and to say thank you, whether you get the job or not. Remembering these three little things will also prevent you from committing those terrible reference blunders that can prevent you from getting a job.

Okay, this is a bad thing to say, but it's hard to find anyone who hasn't "fudged" a little when it comes to references. People... please! If you haven't actually kept in touch with the manager you worked with for three weeks, ten years ago, they're not a suitable reference. And if you actually believe that potential employers will ignore the fact that the telephone numbers you listed for all four of your references are out of service and hire you anyway, think again! Good etiquette applies to references too. In fact, in some cases, references are more important than resumés. Be very careful, your integrity is showing.

Besides the three basics—get permission, let them know someone will be calling, and thank them—here are some other useful tips on how to use good etiquette when providing references:

■ **Get it in writing:** Sometimes it's smart to ask for a written reference first. This provides you with an opportunity to check out a potential reference's communication style and get a feel for how they express themselves. And it saves the reference the time of answering phone calls.

■ **Use discretion:** Make sure it is appropriate for the interviewer to call the reference at their work and specify times when they will actually be available to take calls at home.

■ **Be honest about your relationships:** Don't outright lie or even embellish your relationship with your reference. If you put down a co-worker's name, don't exaggerate and imply that they were somehow your supervisor. Your reference will most likely be caught off guard and you'll be in a lie. It's just bad manners to put someone who's doing you a favor in an awkward position.

■ **Show your gratitude:** You should send a handwritten thank-you card to any reference who received a call from potential employers. If you are hired and an employer mentions that a specific referral was a significant factor in your being hired, you might consider sending a small gift with that thank-you card!

E. Don't blow it now! Tips for following םי

After the interview, good etiquette is still essential. If you gave the interviewer a cell phone or pager number, carry them with you and leave them on. Don't answer the call unless you are able to properly answer questions without distractions or interruptions. Be especially mindful of this if the position you applied for will entail telephone communications with clients. If you answer the phone at home, always use proper telephone etiquette, speak in a polite tone, use full sentences and proper English. "Whattsupp!!!" in your best fraternity voice won't impress potential employers.

If you want to call after an interview is over to find out whether you've gotten the job, take cues from the interviewer as to when a decision will be made or ask the appropriate questions as you leave the interview. If the interviewer suggests that they will call, wait until they do. If the interviewer has indicated that a decision will be made within a week, wait at least a week to call if you don't hear from them first. In spite of what you may think, midnight voicemail messages to the interviewer in desperate voices won't get you the job. Try sending a thank-you card within twenty-four hours of the interview to help keep your name in the back of their mind.

F. You are the company: Etiquette for the interviewer

Employers can benefit from the rules of good etiquette just as surely as their employees can. Use the same rules in an interview setting that you'd use hosting a party at your home. The point is to put people at ease so you can see the type of person you'll be dealing with in a work situation. To accomplish this, an employer should do the following:

- **Location, location!** Pick a good location for the interview and make sure it is reserved. Have a pitcher of water available and make sure the temperature and ventilation in the room are adequate.

- **Make candidates feel comfortable:** Come out from behind the desk and greet interviewees by smiling and shaking their hand. Take a seat beside them rather than across from them; a large desk makes an intimidating physical barrier between you and them that may not bring out the best in this potential employee.

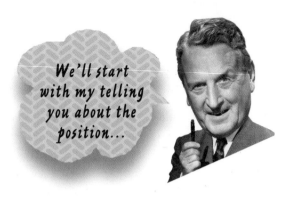

We'll start with my telling you about the position...

- **Remember names:** An employer should actually take a moment to review the resumé of the person with whom they'll be meeting and at least know their name by the time they arrive.

- **Dress well:** Interviewers should be dressed appropriately, according to the company guidelines.

- **Focus:** An interviewee is entitled to the undivided attention of the interviewer for the duration of the interview. Keeping an interviewee waiting, taking calls in their presence, eating lunch at your desk while talking or asking an interviewee to join you on a smoke-break shows disrespect and does not represent any company well. You might also want to avoid distractions like a blinking computer screen and have someone hold your calls entirely during the duration of the interview.

- **Set an agenda:** Nervous interviewees will appreciate an interviewer giving them an "agenda" of sorts outlining the course of the interview. Something like, "we'll start with my telling you about the position, we'll go over your qualifications, and then we'll answer any questions you may have."

- **No surprises please!** There is nothing more intimidating than mentally preparing for a one-on-one interview only to arrive and discover that there is actually a panel reviewing interactive role-playing scenarios. It is respectful to give potential employees all the information they'll need to properly present themselves at the interview.

G. Chapter summary

Competition in modern business is stiff. Both employers and potential employees need to recognize that an ability to show respect and confidence in both business and social situations adds polish and sheen to a well-rounded academic and/or employment record. Employers should be aware that to a potential employee, an interviewer's behavior reflects the integrity, ethics and values of the organization they represent. Potential employees need to understand that first impressions really do matter and busy employers will make hasty judgments about character and ethics based on how an interviewee handles themselves in an interview.

The respect we show others and the respect we have for ourselves must be communicated to others no matter what type of situation we are in. Remember, in business, you're always being interviewed: whether during a scheduled interview, a formal meeting with associates or during lunch with a client. Business people are watching the way you interact with others and how you handle yourself during an initial meeting. Remember to be honest and sincere and keep in mind that a first impression is a lasting one.

Answers to self-assessment quiz

1. **False.** You should tailor your interview clothing to mirror the position you are applying for. For example, if you want to be a corporate executive, don't show up in your khaki's and V-neck sweater. Similarly, chances are the head machinist won't instantly think you suit the part of mechanic if you show up for your interview in a three piece Armani suit. Use your common sense. If you're unsure, call the office in question and ask about their company dress code. If still in doubt, dress up! Better safe than sorry.

2. b) If the interviewer gave "cues" that it would be appropriate to call the next day, do so. Thank the interviewer for their time

and reiterate your interest in the position but don't expect that they've made a decision.

3. **False.** If you have put out applications and anticipate that a potential employer may call, be prepared. Keep your resumé and a list of research or questions by the phone. Answer the phone politely and make sure there is not loud background noise. If you have housemates, ask them to behave accordingly.

4. **False.** It's never smart to hand in anything meant to be a professional document with scribbles, stains or whiteout on it. A resumé helps a potential employer form a first impression of you, make sure it's a good one.

5. **False.** Under no circumstances is it appropriate to answer your cell phone in an interview situation. If you take your pager or cell phone into the room, make sure it's off.

6. **False.** Making the interviewer's job more difficult will not get you points. If you're hard to track down, give them specific times when you can be reached at the numbers provided.

7. **False.** It is very important to maintain your integrity and ethics to the very end of your employ with a company. Have potential new employers call your home and do your job search on your own time.

8. **False.** Unless the interviewer instigates such a conversation, do not namedrop! Nothing is more off-putting than someone who overtly tries to take advantage of close or imagined relationships.

9. **False.** Your comfort is secondary. If you want the job you should dress accordingly.

10. **False.** It's important to have fresh breath, but chewing gum is unsightly and unprofessional. If you have to, you may consider discreetly popping a small mint.

Chapter Three

THE WRITE STUFF:
Written communications

In the modern age, written communications are becoming more and more prevalent with the advent of faxes, emails, and continued reliance on the good old letter. There are etiquette guidelines when we write, just as when we meet someone or speak with them on the phone. Correct protocol for salutations, when and where to send personal cards, how to best write an email, when to include your business card: these are all subtle but important things to know. If you put the wrong salutation on a letter, you're subtly saying "I'm sloppy." If you include a business card in a sympathy gift to an ill business associate, you're saying "I'm tactless." Just like your dress or speech, they won't notice when you do it "write," but doing it wrong will have an effect.

What's your correspondence etiquette IQ? Take the self-assessment and find out.

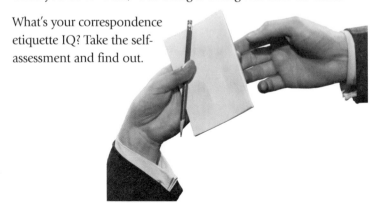

Quiz: Self-assessment

	True or False
1. When you're sending an interesting article or newspaper clipping to a colleague or client it is appropriate to include a business card.	
2. If you want to send an anniversary card to your boss and his wife, you should send it to his home address.	
3. If you are unsure of how a woman wishes to be addressed, it is appropriate to call her directly and ask.	
4. It is appropriate to confirm client meetings via email.	
5. During initial communications with clients, you should use their first and last names plus their title in all communications.	
6. The proper way to close a business letter is: a) "With regard." b) "Affectionately yours." c) "Sincerely." d) "Take care."	
7. In the age of recycling, people are not put off when materials are forwarded to them in "once used" envelopes and packing materials.	
8. It is appropriate to cc under the following circumstances: a) always, to cover your butt. b) only when the recipient's superior will have access to the communication. c) when the communication concerns other parties. d) when the initial recipient does not have relevant authority.	

	True or False
9. When corresponding by fax it is good practice to pre-empt the fax with a telephone call.	
10. When sending an email, it is okay to just sign your name with no address or company information; after all, they can just hit the reply button if they want to communicate with you.	

(See answers at the end of this chapter.)

A. Business correspondence: Say it with style

The business letter is the standard mode of business correspondence, and follows a clear format, up to a point. But style is the key to success in any communication, whether in-person, on the phone, or written. Here are some etiquette tips that can improve your written business communications.

- **Be yourself:** You can follow protocol in terms of how the letter is laid out even if you don't understand why and you can use proper grammar even if you don't always speak properly. But don't use big words that you couldn't possibly use in a sentence and don't exaggerate the formality of your personality by using flowery or overly formal language.

- **Avoid the royal "we":** In business writing it is best to use the first person, that is "I" whenever possible. This is more personal and lends more sincerity than using a collective "we" in the body of a letter that will be written and/or signed by only one person.

- **Echo the writer's style:** Just as you might vary your speech and dress to accommodate your client, you also need to pay attention to the way their written correspondence is communicated. Just as you would respond to a formal letter with a formal letter of your own, if you receive an informal correspondence, even if it's from a boss, client, or co-worker—

you respond in kind. By doing so you convey respect to the reader by saying in not so many words that you understood the mood and tone of their letter and you accept it.

Sending formal correspondence is fairly straightforward but it can be tough to know what to do when you are sending formal business correspondence to someone whom you know personally. If the correspondence relates to a business situation, you need not be too concerned about reiterating a personal relationship. Keep it business-related. The friend will most probably interpret it as a sign of your respect for their professional position. If you feel certain that you must acknowledge the relationship, however, you may consider attaching a short handwritten note along with the letter, or phone ahead to let them know a formal letter is coming.

What happens if you forget your manners when it comes to business correspondence? Well, don't be surprised if you run into one of these correspondence "characters":

THE PRETENTIOUS PENMAN: This "wanna be" Pulitzer Prize-winner can turn a two-sentence thank-you note into a long, drawn-out, flowery ode to friendship that goes on for two pages. It seems apparent that this writer has a lot to say and is having trouble finding someone who wants to listen. You can be sure they had the dictionary and the thesaurus out when they sat down to write, too. Just be grateful they put it in writing and you didn't have to hear it in person.

DEBBIE DROPOUT: Debbie has good intentions, but her inability to spell properly and her failure to abide by even the most simple of grammatical rules leaves readers wondering if her seven-year-old daughter wrote the letter they've just received. In this day and age, sending a word-processed letter without utilizing the spell check is unforgivable. Regardless of the message you're trying to send, the only message received will be "I am careless, uneducated or lazy."

B. When you're this big, they call you Mister! Greetings and salutations

Putting the right greeting on a business letter is not as simple as it may seem. In this day and age, you can't always assume the person you're addressing is a "Mister," and sometimes the name won't tell you. Even if you know it's a woman, do you use Miss, Mrs. or Ms? Due to modern "gender issues" in business and confusion about how to behave in mixed company, there has been a a trend in business writing to forego Mr. Mrs. Miss and Ms altogether. Some people feel strongly that gender should no longer be relevant to business, and so, there is no need to refer to "gender" titles at all. It is now commonplace to see Joe Brown or Joanne Brown on business correspondence. In the past, taking the time to find out what title was appropriate showed that you'd done your homework, but most people now see ignoring these "sub-titles" as a business courtesy and they appreciate that you are not concerned with their marital status.

For business writing it is still appropriate to open a letter with "Dear." This will usually be followed by the person's full name or just the person's first name if the letter is not too formal.

There are special situations where people have special titles. For instance, most of us wouldn't know how to address the mayor if we were seated beside her at a fundraising dinner, let alone how to address a letter to her. In almost every scenario, good business etiquette dictates that you prepare as much as possible. Call the office and find out what the proper address is.

When it comes to closings for business letters, opinions vary. Most often you will still see "Sincerely," which is most appropriate for business. "Yours truly" is okay, but it is more appropriately used in personal letters along with "Very truly yours" or "With affection," and the like. If you have developed a good business relationship with someone and you communicate regularly, you may consider using a closing such as "Respectfully" or "With regard." If there is ever doubt about what closing is appropriate, you may choose to use nothing at all. Simply end the letter with your signature, name and title.

C. Getting it write: Social correspondence in business

Not all business communications are business-related. Sometimes you can be called upon to send a personal card for an occasion, and sometimes it's important to send a thank-you note to someone who's gone above and beyond the call of duty for you. So how do you approach mixed business and social correspondence? Here are some useful tips:

- Business cards do not belong with social correspondence. Whether it's an anniversary card to your boss or a thank-you note to a client, never include your business card.

- Double-check that the letter or card is addressed properly. Use complete, formal names and include titles when available. Always include a return address.

- Get your salutations right. If you do not know whether a woman likes to be addressed as Ms, Miss or Mrs., phone ahead and find out or just use first and last name.

- Try not to use "silly" stationery or cards/envelopes with jokes or characters that could be construed as offensive. Plain is best.

- When writing thank-you cards, do not start the note with, "Thank you…." The note will seem obligatory. Instead, try to highlight the event or occasion or something else positive. Do mention the gift specifically at some point but don't lie. If you really didn't like the vase for example, say, "the vase was a thoughtful gift" instead of "I loved the vase." Sincerity is very important.

- Try to send thank-you notes within 36 hours of the occasion. You may telephone or email thank you's for very casual things or small niceties, however, a written thank you is always better.

- Always RSVP (respond to the invitation). Etiquette dictates that you respond in the same manner as you receive an invitation. That means, if you were invited by phone, you may RSVP by phone. If you received a formal written invitation, you must formally respond in writing.

D. I can't read this! The handwritten note

When was the last time you wrote a note by hand? A card? A letter? Your signature even? In this technological age, handwritten correspondence is indeed a lost art. And when we do have reason to write, who can read it anymore? The etiquette ladies admit that even their handwriting is sometimes illegible. Unfortunately for the stylus-impaired, penmanship is back in fashion. It's pretty easy to bang off a form letter on a computer keyboard or "say it with clipart," but it takes a skilled communicator to get the same message across by hand. The new trends in communicating include monogrammed stationery, luxurious pens, personalized-blended inks, some with fragrance and fancy lettering.

The key to preparing a handwritten note is presentation. Practise good penmanship! The time and energy you spend handwriting is of little value if the receiver cannot read your writing. Choose blue or black ink, space your words and sentences appropriately and remember brevity is key. Also remember that stationery is like clothing. The appearance and quality of the stationery you choose will leave an impression. Do not send correspondence on mismatched, soiled, previously-used or "wrinkled" paper. Finally, remember you're doing it by hand so that the receiver will know this is an original. A photocopy or form letter, handwriting done by computer font, or carbon copy signatures are not personal enough when handwriting is called for. Take time to do it right; you'll be glad you did.

E. 'Tis the season: Special occasion correspondence

What better way to show clients you appreciate their business than by remembering them on special occasions. Holiday greetings show care and consideration for business associates on a personal level. But there are many pitfalls to that sincere, thoughtful touch if you don't take time and care. This is business and that must be remembered even as we try to add a personal note to our working life.

How high is your special occasion IQ? Take the quiz on the following page and find out.

QUIZ: SPECIAL OCCASION CORRESPONDENCE

	True or False
1. An email or phone call is the proper response to a written invitation.	
2. A thank-you note needs to be quite lengthy to be effective.	
3. A form letter is fine as long as your signature concludes the correspondence.	
4. The proper way to address an envelope to a client would include their title, even if it's a greeting card.	
5. After a party, to thank your host, send a thank-you note.	
6. Doodling hearts and smiley faces to finish off the I's in words will add character to greeting messages.	
7. Always call to thank the sender of a thank-you card.	
8. Attach a business card to all correspondence.	
9. A reply to a formal dinner party should be made one week before the event if not stated on invitation.	
10. The majority of people do not mind if you spell their name incorrectly.	

(See answers at the end of this chapter.)

Handwritten messages add a necessary personal touch to seasonal business correspondence. If you want to ensure that your message shows your respect and thoughtfulness towards the recipient, follow these useful pointers on holiday greeting etiquette:

■ **Pick the right card:** Give some thought to the diversity of your client base. Make sure the images and/or greeting on your card are commonplace enough to show respect for the receiver's potential religious customs, beliefs or personal practices.

- **Personalize the message:** If you will be sending cards which have your title, full name or business name embossed or engraved on them, make a point of personalizing the message when you write it and sign your name in your own handwriting at the end. It is in really poor taste to send a social card with a photocopied signature. And you certainly don't want clients to feel they're part of a "bulk" mailing campaign.

- **Address it properly:** If a card is being sent to an associate's place of business, take care when addressing the envelope. If the invitation is strictly business-related and includes both the associate and their spouse, address the envelope to both, with the associate's name first, regardless of gender. Only send a personal card to an associate's office as a last resort. If you must do so, address the envelope to the associate only. Extend the invitation to the associate's spouse inside the card.

- **Remember the family:** If correspondence is being sent to a person's residence, do not assume a wife carries her husband's name nor that a couple is married. Take the time to find out each person's full name. If the couple share a last name, you may use Mr. and Mrs. but don't forget to include the wife's first name. Some generations of women don't mind being addressed as Mr. and Mrs. John Smith but most modern women prefer to see their own name. If the couple do not share a name, simply address the card to both of them, putting the name of the person with whom you have the relationship first and the other person's name second. Remember, etiquette means showing consideration for others, so it is always important to take into account the preference of the addressee when sending correspondence. Always show respect for someone's age and think about what makes them comfortable.

- **Sign it properly:** If you're sending cards on behalf of you and your spouse or someone else, you both should sign the card and the person who is actually doing the writing should sign their name last.

F. This is your life, or is it? Resumé embellishments

A resumé is your first chance to make a good first impression on your new potential employer. However, just because the communication will be in writing rather than spoken, it isn't any less important to tell the truth. After all, if you get the interview, they're going to find out anyway. So avoid any embellishments that can get you into trouble on the interview, or on the job. If you have asked yourself these questions, you're probably stretching the truth.

- How many times can I extend my work dates before anyone one catches on?

- Hmmm, gas station attendant, or was that a petroleum distribution engineer?

- As long as I get most of the details right that will be good enough. The skills I have acquired can be fabricated just a little.

- Is it true that "almost" counts in horseshoes and university courses? After all, I was only three credits short.

- If I helped do the schedule once when the manager got the flu, does that make me an assistant manager or department head?

- Captain of the debating team, volunteer at the hospital, chair for the cheer board, Olympic medalist, goalie for the Toronto Maple Leafs.....oh, come on, there is nothing wrong with a little white lie, is there?

One other important thing to note about resumés is to respect the potential employer's instructions. If it states in the job advertisement that applications should be mailed, absolutely never fax or email them. You may think you'll get noticed by doing it, and believe me, you will. But not in a good way. With email in particular, if you send an unrequested attachment, you will hold up the prospective employer's computer while it downloads. And unrequested attachments often mean someone is sending a virus, for another. Emailing an unrequested attachment is one way to GUARANTEE you will not be considered for employment.

G. Email: The other written correspondence

Because of its speed and convenience, many people equate email correspondence with speech and apply the same rules. Wrong! Email is, in fact, another form of written correspondence. The same writing rules that dictate your formal correspondence still apply, with a little modification. Here are the top ten rules for sending a letter by email:

1. **Salute them.** When it comes to salutations, adhere to the normal guidelines for business correspondence. Pay attention to how a sender refers to himself or herself. For example, if they list their title, you might be wise to list their title when you address a note to them. When in doubt, use formal salutations.

2. **Make Hemingway proud:** Brevity is key. Be concise and to the point.

3. **Don't change the subject:** Include an honest subject heading. Using a misleading subject heading, like "winner," if you are actually soliciting business, will simply annoy or offend your reader.

4. **Get the tone right:** Remember, this isn't a conversation where someone can infer meaning from your tone of voice or gestures. Be very careful with humor and sarcasm, which cannot always be clearly interpreted via email. Write clearly and professionally. Read the message carefully before you send it to check for aspects that could be misconstrued.

5. **Check spelling and grammar:** People read emails the same way they would read a written note. It is not good manners to point out spelling or grammatical errors to senders, but try to send grammatically correct messages yourself.

6. **Sign your message:** Just as you would never send a business letter on plain paper with no letterhead, signature or return address, don't send emails with no identifying information. Every email should include your full name, title, and the company information that would be included in standard letterhead. A file called a "signature" is available in all email programs that allows you to fill all of this information in once and have it automatically included in every email you send.

7. **Reply with care:** There are two important things to note about replies. First, when you send a reply, your signature does not automatically attach itself to the file, so make sure to sign it in full. Secondly, when you reply to an email that has been sent to a group of people either directly or using the cc or blind cc functions, your reply will go to everyone in that group. Make sure you know to whom you're replying!

8. **It's not confidential:** Don't send it by email if you wouldn't post it on the bulletin board. Email administrators always have an option to read emails.

9. **Don't get attached:** Good etiquette dictates that you show caring and consideration for others. When you are attaching a file to an email, it is important to phone ahead to make sure that the other person is expecting it and that it is in a format they can open.

10. **Keep it professional:** Don't waste other people's time sending irrelevant and inconsequential material. A rule of thumb is: if you wouldn't mail it to them, don't email it to them either.

H. Chapter summary

How you write a letter, address an envelope, spell in an email, or determine what to include in fax correspondence, all say as much about your professionalism, self-respect and manners, as do your handshake and speech. Any form of communication plays a part in determining what kind of impression you send. And, first impressions can make or break your business reputation.

Answers to self-assessment:

1. **True.** However, if you are including a handwritten note or have telephoned the recipient in advance, it would be inappropriate to include a business card.

2. **True.** Definitely send the card to the boss's home. Address the card to both the boss and his wife and sign your name. You shouldn't send a card at all unless the boss himself happened to tell you about the anniversary or if you have worked together for a long time and have a "social" as well as professional relationship.

3. **True.** It is absolutely appropriate, in fact recommended that you ask the woman directly or call her office to ensure that you address her properly.

4. **True.** It is appropriate to confirm client meetings by email, particularly if the arrangements were initially made by email. However, keep in mind that email messages are not always accessible, you may also want to leave a voicemail just to be sure.

5. **True.** When you initially meet someone, you should always address them by their formal names. Even if they have given you permission to call them by their first name in person, it's a good idea to use their full name and title in any written correspondence that follows a face-to-face meeting.

6. **c)** It is most appropriate to close a business letter with "Sincerely" but "regards" can sometimes be used. Another alternative is "Respectfully yours."

7. **False.** Although it is becoming commonplace to see "recycled" envelopes and packing materials these days, keep in mind the first impression issue. It might be a good idea to splurge on a new envelope in the beginning and save the recycled papers for ongoing relationships or in-house mail.

8. **c)** You should only cc a letter if your intention is to provide more than one person with the identical correspondence. It is very disrespectful not to notify people when others will be privy to the contents of business communications.

9. **True.** If you are unsure if a person is actually in their office to receive the fax, if the fax is confidential, or if a person shares a fax machine, it's always a good idea to call them first so that they can expect it.

10. **False.** Just as you always send business letters on letterhead with your name and company position identified, you should always include a "signature" on your emails, a file that automatically pops up on all outgoing emails which states your name, position, company and all of the address information included on your company's letterhead.

Answers to special occasion quiz:

1. **False:** The proper way to respond to a written invitation is in writing.

2. **False.** A thank-you note need only be two or three lines of sincere thought.

3. **False.** Any correspondence which is of an emotional nature should be personal and in writing. If you do decide to send a form letter, however, your signature should most certainly be in your own handwriting.

4. **True.** It's a good idea to use someone's title whenever possible. It shows you recognize their accomplishments and respect their position.

5. **False.** It is always more thoughtful to take a moment and send a short, handwritten note.

6. **False.** Unless you're an eight-year-old corporate prodigy, doodles and scribbles including smiley faces are unprofessional and inappropriate.

7. **False.** There is no need to thank someone for thanking you. The thank you's could go on all day.

8. **False.** Under no circumstances should business cards be attached to correspondence of a personal or emotional nature.

9. **False.** Proper etiquette dictates that you RSVP and that you do so as quickly as possible, Most often formal invitations include a "respond by date."

10. **False.** Most people will not cause a scene or correct you even if they do take offence and most people appreciate hearing their name pronounced correctly.

Chapter Four

FACE TO FACE:
Meetings in the
new millennium

No matter how much technology gets developed, the old face-to-face is still where most of our communicating gets done. Meetings are still a standard practice in business—from general office conferences to negotiations to presentations for staff and/or clients—this is where your etiquette pays off. How you present yourself in the meeting as well as before and after it, and even during your bathroom break, can make or break a business deal. So be careful, your manners are showing.

Do you know the basics of modern meetings? Take this quiz and find out.

QUIZ: SELF-ASSESSMENT

	True or False
1. If someone arrives late for a meeting which you are hosting, are you obligated to start over?	
2. You should use agendas to keep people on topic at meetings.	

▶

	True	or	False

3. There is protocol for seating arrangements at meetings, for example, a junior executive who has recently been promoted, shouldn't just plunk themselves down by the boss.

4. If you disagree with the boss during a meeting with co-workers, you should express your opinions openly in front of them.

5. You are often in charge of scheduling meetings over lunch. Your co-workers say you are responsible for providing their lunch if you schedule meetings on their time.

6. If you're attending a meeting with co-workers, it's okay to bring along and answer your cell phone because they all know your business.

7. If a meeting is running late and you have to leave, you should just get up and go.

8. Your attention in meetings is often disrupted by co-workers who whisper, pass notes and fidget. It is appropriate to tell them to pay attention.

9. If you're bored in a meeting and the discussion doesn't pertain to you, you should utilize the time by making notes or sending email on your palm pilot.

10. In a formal meeting, you should always address your boss by her proper name, even if you've worked there for years and are on a first-name basis.

(See answers at the end of this chapter.)

A. Meet me in the boardroom: Meeting etiquette

Isn't it amazing that in this day and age with all the conveniences of modern technology, there still just doesn't seem to be enough time in the day? And just when you think you're catching up, they call a meeting. Countless hours are wasted sitting in poorly lit boardrooms drinking luke-warm coffee and bantering over issues that could have been solved in minutes over the phone. If someone would occasionally take a risk and make a decision about the staff barbecue, the quantity of paper being wasted or the style of company nametags, we could all get on to the business of doing business.

Believe it or not, using basic etiquette is a sure-fire way to make the most of a meeting. The number one rule of etiquette is to show consideration for others. If you remember this rule, the rest will follow. Here are some examples of how etiquette can work for you the next time you plan a meeting.

- **Be on time:** If you respect others, you respect that their time is valuable, so be sure to start and finish the meeting on time. If some attendees are late, begin without them. Some experts suggest that scheduling meetings toward the end of the day or just prior to scheduled lunches or breaks is added incentive for people to show up on time and close the meeting quickly.

- **Stick to the issues:** Decide ahead of time what absolutely must be covered and plan your agenda accordingly. Let attendees know in advance if there are issues for which they need to be prepared. Do not stray from the agenda.

- **Lead by example:** Whether you are leading the meeting or attending it, show up on time, be prepared, have a positive attitude, be courteous and speak clearly. Others will follow your lead.

- **Hold questions:** At the beginning of the meeting, ask attendees to hold their questions until the end of the meeting. Often questions will answer themselves as the meeting progresses.

- **No cell phones:** Remind attendees to turn off cell phones and pagers, no need for rude interruptions.

- **Be specific:** Summarize the issues and decisions before the meeting concludes and follow up with a formal memorandum the day after the meeting. Be sure to reiterate any action to be taken and set specific follow-up dates.

- **Place food carefully:** If you will be providing food service during the meeting, be sure it is placed properly so that attendees may help themselves without interrupting the meeting.

- **Give them a break:** Provide breaks and beverages for long meetings. Thirsty, tired people can often lose their concentration and guarantee a meeting goes over-time. If the meeting exceeds 45 minutes, ensure that beverages are available or notify attendees to bring a beverage. If it exceeds one hour, offer attendees a short break period every hour.

B. Show me the money, or a portion thereof: Negotiations

In a perfect business world the contract or proposal submitted to your client would be promptly signed and couriered back to the office complete with deposit check. But in the real world, this rarely happens, which is why negotiating is a huge part of everyday business dealings. To accomplish the goals set out for you and your company, you must remember to bring your manners along with you and keep in mind that the way you conduct yourself can make or break the deal.

The most important thing to remember in a negotiation is what its very name implies, give and take. You go in with an understanding of how low you will go, start high, and work your way down. Each party responds to the other and you're both working towards a result that will please, or at least appease, both parties.

Basic etiquette dictates that you show the other party respect. That means not wasting their time—be punctual, come prepared, make sure you researched their company so you don't ask needless questions. Greet everyone, no matter what their status. Be consistent and calm in your presentation. Consistent voice, manner and style shows dependability while emotionality indicates reckless impulsiveness. Listen to people without interrupting and respond to what they are saying; don't consistently hammer home your own point and don't ignore or debate their opinions. Simply say what you mean to say clearly and check to make sure you're being understood.

If you treat others with respect in any situation, even a heated debate, you will come out the winner in the end.

C. It's all in the delivery: Making presentations

Ask almost anyone and they'll tell you that one of the things people are most afraid of is speaking in front of others. Even those of us who teach or train for a living still have nervous moments. When doing business, presentations are often a part of the job— from making a pitch to a group of clients to presenting new ideas to your co-workers. Taking the floor is always nerve-wracking, but etiquette can help you build your corporate confidence and present with ease.

Now, this is a blackboard and soon I'm going to put something on it.

When it comes to making presentations, nothing is more important than exuding confidence. The etiquette ladies have learned that there are five main areas for projecting confidence in a presentation.

- **Know your stuff:** If you know what you're doing, you'll automatically be more confident in making your presentation. Make sure you've thought the material through and have researched every angle so you're not blind-sided by questions you cannot answer. It doesn't matter how well you speak or how charming and respected you are if the content of your speech or presentation does not accomplish your goal. Materials have to be relevant. Know your client or group and tailor your materials to their needs; don't make assumptions about what people know, make sure your information is clear and concise. One final note of advice, time yourself. It is extremely disrespectful to run late, particularly if another presenter is to follow.

- **Speak slowly:** One of the most common mistakes novice speakers make is speaking too quickly. Typically they start out faster and as they get less nervous or notice the audience is attentive, they will slow down a little. Take a deep breath and make an effort to speak slowly and deliberately. Take pauses to allow your audience to catch up. Pronounce your words carefully. Try to resist dropping the "ing" at the end of words, leave out slang and short form words, and watch that your voice doesn't trail off towards the end of sentences. Volume should be consistent.

- **Make eye contact:** As you deliver your presentation, make direct and varied eye contact. Shift your view from the front to the back and sides of the room whenever possible. Try to make direct eye contact with someone important in the audience, like the CEO or person in charge, but don't hold their gaze too long.

- **Watch your body language:** Studies show that up to 50 per cent of the message you send in a public presentation is through non-verbal communication. Practise your speech in front of the mirror or have someone observe you. Notice if you have a tendency to nod your head too much or any other quirks or ticks you might have. Watch that you are standing tall and exuding confidence. Be careful not to fidget and, whenever possible, let the audience see your hands. People seem to trust speakers more when they can see their hands.

- **Rehearse:** Just as you must rewrite several drafts of a document to get it right, rehearsing is the key to making a good presentation. Regardless of how many times you've previously presented the material or how well you think you know the crowd or the material, practise! Your delivery will improve every time you rehearse, the incidence of "um" and "huh" will hopefully decrease and, with increasing comfort, you will be able to present your material with grace, humor and confidence. Oddly enough, the more you rehearse, the less rehearsed your speech will seem to the audience.

There's a lot you can do to build your own confidence in a presentation setting but sometimes the reactions of your audience are beyond your control. Yawns, interruptions, and inappropriate questions happen, but if you exude confidence you can downplay a lot of this behavior. Remember, stay cool, and present your material as clearly as possible, especially when you meet characters like these ones:

ONE-UP WALLY: It does not matter how wonderful your idea is Mr.One-up will have a better one. He is so intelligent that he has a better idea than yours, even before he's heard yours. Eventually this poor soul will end up sitting alone. Oh Wally, will you ever learn?

Bravo!
Author!
Author!

BANDWAGON BOB: It starts out as simple head nodding, appreciative smiles and the occasional audible "uh hmm." Then before you know it, the biggest fan you've never met is applauding when you least expect it or showing approval by too much heartfelt, long-winded laughter at the slightest joke. It's going to be difficult convincing the program organizers that you've never met him before and that you didn't pay him to come along for support. Sit down Bob and keep quiet!

If you find yourself with an interruptor in the crowd, talk to the person during a break and explain that you appreciate their comments but would rather hear them after the presentation when you can give them your full attention. If the interruptions continue, you may be forced to address them during the presentation. Take a deep breath, pause for a moment, and then politely ask this person to give you a chance to finish. Try something like: "Wally, I am very interested in your feedback, and in ten minutes I will complete my presentation and will receive questions and comments." Be polite yet firm.

D. From the boardroom to the bathroom: Washroom etiquette

How one behaves in the privacy of his or her own home is, and should remain, their own business. When it comes to public restrooms, however, personal and sometimes quirky private behaviors suddenly become very inappropriate. This is especially true of workplace washrooms.

When it comes to manners, no place is off limits. If you want to present a professional competent image you have to be consistent. The poise and polish you exhibit in the boardroom will be of little consequence if an underling overhears you bashing the boss in what you thought was a "private" corporate bathroom. Just a reminder, when it comes to work; any speaking you do is "public speaking" and that includes talking in the biffy.

Here are the top ten tips on how to keep your public washroom "business" more private.

1. **Neither a borrower...** Don't borrow from others when in the washroom. This applies to reading materials, make-up, hairbrushes and toiletries. First and foremost, asking to borrow personal objects from others is not at all hygienic. And secondly, even people who say yes to lending are almost always very uncomfortable about it.

2. **Mind your own business:** Don't peek under stalls or through the crack in the door. Don't stare at others or watch them while in the washroom, and don't strike up casual conversations with the person in the stall next to you.

3. **It's not a dining room:** Don't bring food or drink into the washroom. You'd be surprised how many people do this. Even worse, don't ask someone to hold your stuff while in the washroom.

4. **Keep it brief:** People often lose track of time in the washroom and it's rude to keep others waiting.

5. **Do not talk on the phone:** There is nothing worse than the sound of flushing and other bathroom noises in the background, let alone knowing someone has their pants around their ankles while they're talking to you on the phone.

6. **Flush, check the bowl and then flush again:** There are some things no one needs to see.

7. **Clean up after yourself:** If there was a mess when you got there, or you made one that you cannot clean up, call someone who can. Use the receptacles which have supplies, wipe the seat, floor, walls or door if you made a mess, and WASH YOUR HANDS. Don't forget, clients often use company bathrooms too.

8. **Everyone knows why you're there:** Do not waste water by flushing excessively or running the tap to disguise normal bathroom noises. Polite people will not brag about the noises they make nor will they comment on the noises of others.

9. **Keep your private business private:** People have a tendency to discuss very private things related to bodily functions and health issues in the bathroom. Don't do it! You never know who's in the next stall.

10. **Stick to your own:** No matter how long the line up, men and women should not sneak into the washroom designated for the opposite sex. Too many surprises.

E. Chapter summary

In spite of all the technological advancements in the modern business world, we cannot rely on technology to adequately communicate all the nuances of human interaction. More and more we're required to understand the rules for conduct in face-to-face communications. Knowing how to conduct yourself in meetings, in negotiations, when giving presentations, and even in the bathroom, are important aspects of building your Ps & Qs for profit.

Answers to self-assessment

1. **False:** Let them catch up on their own time unless their contribution is vital to the next stage of the meeting.

2. **True.** Always send an agenda in advance of the meeting if possible and preface the meeting by giving guidelines as to the order and timing of questions. In addition, it is always a good idea to send a follow-up memo to the meeting attendees that summarizes the meeting and gives suggestions for preparing for the next one.

3. **True.** Meeting protocol is as follows: Whoever is leading the meeting sits at the head of the table or to the right of the highest-ranking person attending the meeting. If there is a guest at the meeting, they should be seated to the right of the highest-ranking person. Typically, whoever is taking minutes, sits to the left of the meeting host. The next in rank sits to their right and so on, down to the lowest-ranking person. Some companies have organizational charts which dictate who sits where. If there is no established protocol, wait until the host or highest ranking person says where to sit.

4. **False.** Even when you are asked to give an opinion, refrain from doing so if you will embarrass a higher-up. Diplomacy is key. Keep controversial opinions to yourself when in a group; they are better discussed in private sessions with the boss. Sometimes when higher-ups request opinions and ideas in a group setting, this is merely a courtesy and you should not respond.

5. **False.** Check with your boss and/or your human resource department as to company policy. If the meeting is called at the last minute, it would be a nice gesture to provide something to eat, even if you expect attendees to pay a small fee.

6. **False.** If your full attention is required and expected in a meeting, regardless of who the meeting is with, you should not bring your cell phone.

7. **False.** If you know you have to leave at a specific time, tell whoever is leading the meeting in the beginning. Just getting up and going is very rude and may be seen as insubordinate or disrespectful.

8. **False.** Unless you're their supervisor, leave the scolding to whoever is in charge of the meeting. Make a point of changing seats next time.

9. **False.** Using a palm pilot while someone is speaking is as rude as making a call on your cell phone. Do your best to stay interested in the subject at hand.

10. **True.** If you feel strongly about this, discuss it with your boss, but in most cases, it is preferable to refer to the boss as Mr. Boss. This shows respect in front of new employees, clients, and guests who may be unaware of, offended by, or intimidated by a "first-name" reference to your boss in a formal meeting situation.

Chapter Five

BLENDED, SHAKEN AND STIRRED: Mixing business with pleasure

I n modern business, much communication happens in social settings. There's nothing more confusing than knowing how to act in an environment that's not an office, but not a personal social setting either. Whether it's a cocktail party, a business luncheon, an office party, a lunch interview or any other situation that's not strictly "at the office" (like the washroom, the elevator, the lobby), there are rules for behaving when we're with the "people from work."

So, how good is your social etiquette? Take the quiz on the following page and find out.

QUIZ: SELF-ASSESSMENT

	True	or	False

1. If you are visiting someone's home for the first time, you are required to bring a small gift.

2. When you meet someone for the first time, you should stand, smile, shake their hand, introduce yourself, and:
a) sit down
b) start talking about the weather
c) say hello
d) give them your card

3. Always request an ashtray if you are a smoker and an ashtray has not been provided.

4. Even if you said thank you in person when you received a gift, you still have to send a written thank-you card.

5. RSVP stands for:
a) reasonable service provided
b) respondez vous s'il vous plait
c) return sender very expensive presents
d) respond soon if you cannot come

6. At a formal event, a man need not wear a tie.

7. If your cell phone goes off in the middle of your lunch at a local restaurant, you should:
a) answer it but be brief
b) immediately shut if off
c) ignore it and let it ring
d) apologize and leave the table to take the call, if you must

	True	or	False
8. Chewing gum is a very good habit to get into if you want to keep your breath fresh.			
9. A good handshaker maintains hand-to-hand contact until an introduction is complete.			
10. If you're on the phone and your call waiting beeps, you should:			
a) ignore the beep and let the call go to voicemail			
a) ask the person you are speaking to if they will hold for a minute, click to the next person and say you'll call back			
a) just put the first caller on hold and take the second call			
a) quickly get rid of the first caller and take the second call			

(See answers at the end of this chapter.)

A. Dining 101: Basic business dining

Whether you're meeting your interviewer over lunch or entertaining a client at dinner, you'll be expected to conduct yourself properly. Certainly, dining etiquette has as much to do with the art of conversation as it does with which fork to use, but no one will hear what you're saying if they're distracted by the tomato sauce on your cheek or the slurping noises you make with your soup. Once again, modern manners are about showing respect and consideration for others. Making others comfortable is the most important thing.

Now, we all know the rules of dining etiquette—never talk with your mouth full, sit up straight with your feet flat on the floor, leave the table if you have to blow your nose or pick your teeth, don't let your utensils touch the table, don't make a scene if you burp or sneeze, etc.—but there are a few other things important to remember for business dining in particular:

- Do not talk business until the meal is complete. Your meal should be enjoyed and conversation should be positive and appropriate. This is the time you spend developing a relationship and getting acquainted.

- Pace yourself so that everyone finishes at the same time— then you can get down to business.

- Remember to turn off all cell phones and pagers. The most important people are the ones sitting in front of you. If you answer a phone call and discuss other business in front of them, the deal may be over before it began.

- No matter how many times you ask "do you mind if I smoke?" Most people will tell you they don't. That's because most of them are just too polite to say so. Smoke outside, in the lounge, or wait until you get back to your office.

- Don't fidget! Keep your hands in your lap when you're not eating. Nervous gestures are distracting.

- Most importantly for business dining, be sure to keep the conversation on "appropriate topics." Avoid the three biggies—politics, religion and sex—but also avoid personal topics like health, diet, and problems; don't gossip; be careful with humor as some jokes can be taken as offensive; and never, never talk about money, not even that amazing deal you just got on your new car!

Let's test your knowledge of business dining etiquette. Read the following scenarios and think about how you would handle each situation.

Quiz: Business Dining

1. What should you do if you're at a formal dinner and the person beside you takes your bread plate by mistake?

2. Your boss always orders these huge, greasy meals for everyone when you have luncheon meetings. You hate fatty food and would never order it for yourself. He's paying; do you have to eat it?

3. You're hosting a lunch meeting and you want to make a good impression. Would you sit with your back to the wall or facing the door?

4. You have a key client who continually answers her cell phone during your meetings, especially at lunch. Sometimes you just want to yank the phone out of her hands. How do you tell her it's rude and that you're not impressed with her?

(See answers at the end of this chapter.)

B. The power lunch: What to do when you're the host

Just like hosting a meeting, hosting a power lunch means setting the standard for your guests, and good etiquette means showing care and consideration for others. The key to hosting a power lunch is preparation. Make sure you know as much about your guests as possible, be at the restaurant early and be waiting at the door to escort guests to the table, have a seating arrangement in mind, make arrangements ahead of time to settle the bill so a check won't be brought to the table, know if a client is a smoker and find out their preference before-hand, and, finally, pre-order the lunch if time is of the essence and make sure you check with guests about food allergies or preferences.

The other important thing to remember about hosting a lunch is to mind your manners. Don't talk business during the meal unless you've agreed to before-hand, have an agenda prepared to show the client you respect their valuable time, escort guests to the door after the meal and thank them for their time, and send a thank-you note to each of the guests afterwards. Most importantly, don't make comments if you're unhappy with the restaurant. Avoid the problem altogether by choosing a restaurant you already know. Exceptional dining experiences linger in the minds of potential clients and give you the chance to concentrate on being an efficient and confident host.

C. Tips on tipping: Paying the bill includes gratuities

Business etiquette experts agree that everyone deserves to experience your good manners, including your server. Just because you're tipping them does not mean you have the right to be rude. Whether it's your hairdresser, the bellman, the taxi driver or your golf caddy, say "please," "thank you" and "excuse me" when appropriate, in addition to leaving a tip, and don't forget to smile and make eye contact.

Here are some guidelines on tipping. Don't forget, etiquette is situational. The most important thing to remember about gratuities is set reasonable standards and be consistent in recognizing them:

- Don't feel bullied to leave a tip if you were not impressed with the service. Some view tips as a "thank-you" gift for services rendered and others view it as an inducement for continued good service. Whatever your motives for tipping are, be consistent and plan to tip based on these motives.

- The host, meaning whoever is making the arrangements, should take care of the bill and leave the tip. If the bill is split, the gratuity is also split.

- If you are a guest of the host and you receive some extra special personal service, you may leave a tip unless you have been told in advance that it has been taken care of.

- Do not cause a scene or force a gratuity on someone who expresses discomfort about accepting a tip. Some employers have strict guidelines regarding the acceptance of tips.

- If you are traveling abroad, find out in advance what the local tipping customs are.

- If gratuities are included in the billing, no additional tip is required.

D. Don't be a cocktail weenie: Business receptions

Believe it or not, it is bad manners to park yourself by the shrimp tree at a cocktail reception and hope that someone interesting will approach you while you're stuffing your face. You may also be surprised to know that you probably won't meet many potential clients if you linger on the sidelines all night with your co-workers.

There probably isn't an adult alive who isn't nervous when entering a room full of strangers. Confidence, or at least looking confident, is key. Walk into a room with purpose, make direct eye contact and smile at strangers as you pass by. Chances are they'll approach you before you have to worry about how to approach them.

Receptions are opportunities to make a "hit," to borrow a term from marketing. The more people are exposed to something—like an advertisement for a product, a song, or you!—the more likely they are to remember it. Marketing wisdom suggests that three "hits" will implant an idea in people's mind. Your appearance at a business reception is your chance to make one "hit," and it's a big one. People remember someone they've met in person far better than a name on a letter or a voice on the phone.

The most important thing to do is get out there and introduce yourself. Choose the people you want to meet carefully and use your best etiquette skills—including listening, never interrupting, shaking hands, etc.—to introduce yourself to them. There's no need to talk business other than to let them know who you are and what your company does. If they want to know more, they'll ask! Be respectful of their time and attention and, if they give you a card, read it and ask them a few questions. All the social skills described in earlier chapters come into play here and will be available in your hour of need if you practise them regularly!

E. There's got to be a morning after: Party tips for the working world

Whether you're inviting others to your home or you expect to be invited to the home of others, whether you're attending a reception at the office, a hotel or a restaurant—if it involves work associates, it's still business, and the rules still apply. We can all readily recount stories where business turned to pleasure as the night grew late and the lights grew dim, stories where professionals found themselves over-indulging in alcoholic punch or wearing a lamp shade and little else, not to mention the things they did and don't remember. You can be guaranteed that everyone else will remember, and don't be surprised if you're not on the guest list next year. Whether you're the host or the guest, there are etiquette guidelines that if followed, help everyone keep their self-respect and their jobs. Remember, there's got to be a morning after.

Here are the basic ten rules to follow when planning or attending work-related parties:

1. The "theme" or "mood" of a party should be clearly stated on the invitation. This helps guests avoid the humiliation of showing up in their best sequined dress, only to find everyone else in jeans. And if your invitation clearly states "formal," you're not doing anyone else a favor by ignoring these directions. You may not care, but others, certainly the host, will.

2. Invitations should also suggest what services will be provided. Countless times, we've starved ourselves all day, saving our appetites for the dinner party, and all that was served was crackers and cheese. It's hard to fill up on olives and it's hard to look attractive while wrenching with hunger pains.

3. If the occasion requires substantial planning and preparation, you can expect the host to call you if you're tardy in sending back the RSVP. It is very commonplace these days to receive "regrets only" cards with seasonal invitations. This means that the recipient of the card need only respond if they definitely cannot attend, otherwise, it is assumed that they will attend the function. This works well for less formal or come-and-go scenarios where the host doesn't require a firm number of RSVPs to make arrangements.

4. "Spouses welcome" doesn't always allow for all "significant others" to attend or that you can bring your brother or six-year-old daughter as a date. Check with the host. And, if you are the host, don't presumé that the spouse or significant other you may have met last year is the same one you'll meet this year. If it's not, don't ask questions. It's none of your business.

5. If you have been invited to someone's home, bring something. If the invitation states something specific, like BYOB, don't show up empty-handed. If you're not sure what to bring, call and ask the host or take a non-food item, like flowers, candles or even a disposable camera with a bow. If

you do take food or beverage items, keep in mind that the host is not required to serve them and you shouldn't take the left-over items home—including half a bottle of vodka—unless the host suggests you do.

6. If you are invited to a restaurant, do not order the most expensive dish unless the host hints that it is acceptable. Often a host will comment on a specific menu item; pay attention, typically, the price attached to this item suggests the dollar range the host anticipated spending. If in doubt, choose something in the middle of the menu price range. Choosing the most inexpensive item can also be insulting to the host.

7. If a restaurant meal has been prearranged, don't cause a fuss if you are unhappy with the meal choice. Keep in mind that the host has a difficult job keeping everyone happy.

8. When you arrive at your designated table, extend your hand and greet your tablemates. Don't despair if you've been seated between the office buffoon and the co-worker you hate—you're only obligated to sit with them through dinner, and then you're free to mingle. If the people at the table are new to you, try to make them feel welcome. And remember, unless the meal has been designated a business dinner, do not discuss business.

9. Sometimes people have a couple of drinks and the topics of conversation become a free for all. Remember the rule: "Say it in your head, see if it sounds appropriate, and only then, say it out loud." Even after a couple of beers, telling the boss's wife you have drapes made of the same fabric as her dress shouldn't sound appropriate in your head or out loud.

10. Most importantly, do not overindulge. If you cannot be sure you will behave appropriately under the influence, monitor your alcoholic intake carefully. Keep in mind, it may be a social evening, but you'll have to look those people in the eye from across the boardroom table tomorrow.

So what happens if you forget your business etiquette in a social situation? It's not always fatal but here are some examples of the types of characters that emerge when we confuse pleasure with business:

GOOD TIME CHARLIE: There's one in every crowd. All he wants to do is party down, man! Hey, don't leave yet, the party is just getting started. Why is it that the quiet guy from shipping chooses the staff party night to come out of his shell? He'll be the last to leave and you can be sure he'll borrow something from the host bar on his way out. He'll be feeling it tomorrow and the shipping department will never be the same.

MARTHA STEWARD: Anything you, the hotel, the server, the host or even the guest of honor can do, Martha can do it better. She organizes the office—that's her job—and she's taken it upon herself to organize the party. While everyone else is enjoying their salad, she'll be refolding napkins or wiping down the wall behind the podium. Martha will make sure your meal is cut into small pieces and that you take home the gardenia's from the bathroom—the company paid for them after all.

Now fold your napkin precisely 18 centimetres.

F. Making a list, checking it twice: The art of giving and receiving gifts

Shopping for family is hard enough, never mind "giving at the office." What do you have to contend with at your workplace? Another year of five-dollar gag gifts? The picky boss who has everything? The cheap co-worker who "re-gifts?" Maybe the theme is "pink" this year, or maybe everyone's making homemade gifts. It's not always easy to give cheerfully under these circumstances, but if you want to keep the peace at work, you'll have to grin and bear it.

The first and most important question is what do you buy the boss? This one's tricky. You don't want to be too personal, but you want your gift to reflect your personal relationship. You don't want to look like a brown-noser by spending a fortune, but you want your thoughtfulness to be noticed. What to do, what to do? Even if you've worked at the office for a long time and have a good personal and professional relationship with the boss, it's best to get together with your co-workers and give the boss a gift as a group. Choose something impersonal. Don't give him or her flannel pajamas or bubble bath. Stick to books, artwork, edibles, or movie or theater passes.

How do you handle all those other awkward moments? What are the modern rules for giving and receiving gifts? Here are some tips to help you through the holidays.

When giving gifts:

■   Stay within the predetermined budget. Don't spend less. You'll look cheap. Don't spend more. The receiver will feel uncomfortable.

■   Do take a moment to wrap the gift. Giving gifts wrapped in obviously re-cycled paper or comic pages looks careless.

■   If you plan to give to some co-workers and not to others, do so in private. Hurt feelings can linger throughout the year. It's also a good idea to have a couple of extra "generic" gifts (candy, candles, books) on hand just in case you're surprised by a co-worker's gift and feel the need to reciprocate.

- Don't give liquor. Some people are offended by alcoholic gifts so it's best to err on the side of caution.

- Think twice before you buy that book of dirty jokes, the blow-up doll, or have last year's secret convention photos ironed onto T-shirts. It's never good manners to deliberately embarrass or humiliate someone. Put yourself in their shoes.

When receiving gifts:

- Always try to open the gift as soon as it is given while the person who gave it is present.

- Smile, accept graciously and say thank you.

- Once a gift has been opened, do not "trade" it with a co-worker for something you prefer unless switching is part of an anonymous exchange. And certainly don't trade in front of the giver if you know who it is.

- Try to avoid talking negatively about the gifts you receive. You never know who helped choose the gift and negative comments have a tendency to be passed around the office.

- If you are uncomfortable with a gift—maybe it is too expensive or seems inappropriate—talk to the giver in private. You shouldn't accept gifts from anyone if doing so obligates you in some way that makes you uncomfortable.

- Always send a written thank you for very thoughtful or unexpected gifts.

- If the gift was unexpected on your part, you are not expected to rush out and get a gift of equal value for the giver.

G. Chapter summary

Rules, rules, rules! No wonder we have difficulty keeping it all straight. Whether it's a business scenario, a social event or a situation mixing the two, the basic guidelines are the same: think about what impression you'll be sending by your actions and think about whether you're showing care and consideration for others.

Answers to self-assessment

1. **True.** It is never courteous to show up at someone's home empty-handed. Try to take along something small like flowers, fruit, or candy, or you may bring along a bottle of wine, bottled water, or soft drinks. If you are caught off-guard and must go with nothing, send a small gift along with a thank-you card the following day.

2. **c)** Stand, smile, shake their hand, introduce yourself and say hello!

3. **False.** Sometimes the absence of an ashtray is a silent signal that smoking is not appreciated. If you must smoke, excuse yourself and go to a lobby, smoking room, or outdoors.

4. **False.** It is not necessary to send a card if you said thank you in person, however, it's nice to do so if the gift was especially thoughtful, unexpected or extravagant.

5. **b)** RSVP stands for "respondez vous s'il vous plait" which is loosely translated as "please respond."

6. **False.** A man should wear a tie and a jacket to a formal event. Most often "black or white tie" will be indicated on a formal invitation referring to a tuxedo being required.

7. **b)** Immediately shut it off and most certainly apologize. Whatever you do, don't answer it.

8. **False.** Chewing gum is an unsightly and impolite behavior. Try mints instead.

9. **False.** A good handshaker maintains eye contact until the introduction is complete but they break hand contact after three or four quick pumps.

10. **b)** Ask the person you are speaking to if they mind holding, switch to the second call, take a message, and return to the first caller as soon as possible.

Answers to dining etiquette quiz:

1. There will always be someone at the table who doesn't know the rules. Proper etiquette dictates that you should not say anything, unless you know them well enough to make a joke. Instead, ask the service attendant to bring you another plate. This is preferable to taking the wrong plate as well and everyone at the table getting mixed up.

2. It is polite not to wrinkle your face or comment to the host, especially in front of others. However, you might consider speaking to the boss in private. Tell him how much you appreciate the gesture and that you recognize he's paying, but would he mind terribly if you ordered for yourself— something of the same or lesser value, of course. The other option would be to call the restaurant ahead of time, explain the situation, and have them substitute something preferable when they bring your plate.

3. The position of power depends entirely on where you are, the business at hand, and who the guests are. You should always give the guests the most comfortable position, seat guests who need to converse together beside each other, and seat yourself so that your guests can look at you and listen without the distraction of a noisy kitchen or picture window. Most often, the host will sit facing the door.

4. You have encountered a very common problem. In any social setting, the person you are face-to-face with should always be the most important person. First try subtlety, make a point of commenting, "I'll just shut my cell phone off so we are not rudely interrupted during our meeting." If that doesn't work, tell her outright that you would appreciate her undivided attention and that you find her cell phone distracting. People should know better!

Conclusion

When it comes to modern business, developing superior communication skills and presenting yourself positively will ensure that you obtain and keep both your dream job and key clients. Remember that you're always being interviewed. The basic words you say, to your body language, to the way you write, meet, or interact in social situations, good old-fashioned etiquette is the key to making that subtle difference between being a competent employee to an exceptional one. Minding your P's and Q's will positively affect your bottom line and you will surely profit.

Acknowledgements:

A special thank-you to Suzanne Gallant for her illustrative talents to these books.

A warm thanks to Esther Bast, Bill Steele, Dorothy Cadorath and Christine Van Cauwenberghe.

About us:

"In Good Company" is a Winnipeg based full service etiquette company. The business originated in 1999 with co-founders Karen Mallett and Lewena Bayer. The timing couldn't have been better and "In Good Company" offers keynote addresses, executive training, social and dining workshops and a variety of children's etiquette programs, including Courtesy Camp. Visit them on the web at www.etiquetteladies.com